Life Lessons from our kitchen to your's.

ISBN:

9781088180730 (sc)

Illustrations by Frances Rose Español

Layout and Design by Louie Romares

Exceptionally Ezra

And the Father's Day Fiasco

Written by: Taylor Harper

Illustrated by: Frances Rose Español

To our little boys —
it is truly a gift being
your mom

Ezra is a boy.

He loves to cook.

And on this particular day... he awoke in a panic.

... because

today was Father's Day.

But what could he do?

Bake him a cake!

So he went to get
his ingredients.

First, he added the mix.

Next, he added the eggs, but just two.

And it only got worse from there.

That looks close enough.

Then it was time to mix.

Into the oven.

Now, what was it supposed to be at again?

He was soon met with an unwelcome surprise.

Ezra wanted a cake, not a mess.

Mom said, "How would you feel if we made one together?"

Ezra figured Mom could help.

Mom suggested they clean up the mess first.

Mom: First, we put the mix in the bowl...

then add three eggs.

Mom: Now, two tablespoons of butter.

Ezra: I didn't measure it last time...
but it looked close enough.

Ezra: Time to mix?

Mom: Yes,
time to mix.

Now it was time for the oven.

Ezra: I thought it would be ok.

Mom: Come sit down with me while our cake bakes.

Ezra: Ok, Mom.

Mom: Ezra, rules make things fun. They are there to help you.

Ezra: You're right, Mom. I should have followed the directions.

Mom: Now how about we take the cake out and decorate it for Dad?

Ezra: That sounds like a good idea.

Dad: Wow, it looks like you two had a lot of fun today.

Mom: Yes, we did.

Ezra: I learned that rules can make things fun and, if you need help, it's ok to ask!

EZRA'S FAMOUS FATHER'S DAY CAKE

Ingredients

Buttercream

1 lb unsalted butter softened to room temperature (453g)
¼ teaspoon salt
6 cups powdered sugar (750g)
6 Tbsp heavy cream or milk of choice
2 teaspoons vanilla extract

Cake

9 Tablespoons unsalted butter softened
3 cups granulated sugar (600g)
1 cup canola oil vegetable oil would also work (236ml)
4 teaspoons vanilla extract
4 cups+ 2 Tbsp all-purpose flour (all of the flour goes into the cake batter, you will also need additional flour for preparing the cake pan) (516g)
4 ½ teaspoons baking powder
1 ½ teaspoons salt
1 1/2 cup milk (355ml)
9 egg whites room temperature preferred
2 cups sprinkles" (80g)

Method

1. Preheat oven to 350F (175C) and prepare 3 8-inch round cake pans by generously greasing and flouring. Be sure to shake out excess flour.
2. In stand mixer, beat butter on medium-low speed until creamy.
3. Add sugar and oil and beat until all ingredients are well-combined and creamy.
4.Scrape down the sides and bottom of the bowl and then stir in your vanilla.
5. In separate bowl, whisk together your flour, baking powder, and salt.
6. Measure out your milk.
7. With mixer on medium speed, gradually alternate between adding the flour mixture and the milk to the butter mixture, starting and ending with the flour mixture. Stir until each one is almost completely combined before adding the next.
8. Pause occasionally to scrape down sides and bottom of bowl.
9. In separate bowl, combine your egg whites and, with a hand-mixer on high-speed, beat until stiff peaks form.
10. Using a spatula, gently fold your egg whites and sprinkles into your batter. Take care to scrape the sides and bottom of the bowl so that ingredients are well-combined, and take care not to over-mix.
11. Evenly divide cake batter into prepared pans.
12. Bake on 350F (175C) for 35-40 minutes, or until a toothpick inserted in the center of each cake layer comes out clean or with few crumbs (should not be wet). For best results, rotate your cake pans halfway through baking to ensure even baking.
13. Cakes will be a light golden brown when done baking.
14. Remove cakes from oven and allow to cool for 15 minutes. Run a butterknife around the inside rim of each pan and invert each onto a cooling rack.
15. Allow to cool completely before frosting.

Frosting

In stand mixer, beat butter on medium-speed until creamy.

- Add salt and beat again for about 20 seconds.
- Gradually, about 1 cup at a time, add powdered sugar, waiting until each cup is completely mixed before adding the next cup.
- Tbsp at a time, add the heavy cream on medium-high speed, waiting until each addition is well-combined before adding the next 2 Tbsp.
- Add flavoring (vanilla extract or emulsion), and stir on medium-high for 30 seconds.

Transfer one layer of your cooled cake to serving platter. Use frosting to ice the top. Add the next layer, ice the top of that. Add your third layer on top and ice the top, and then do a thin "crumb coating" around the entire cake.

- Transfer to freezer for 10-15 minutes, then remove and apply a clean, thick coat of frosting around the entire cake.

www.ingramcontent.com/pod-product-compliance
Ingram Content Group UK Ltd.
Pitfield, Milton Keynes, MK11 3LW, UK
UKHW061032310726
14089UKWH00009B/212
9781088180730

While attending school, David notices lots of kids performing various activities.

EXIT

Opie was the swimming champion for two years straight. He is so fast, I believe he can beat a baby dolphin! Maybe my imagination is getting away with me . . .

Chipmunk is the captain of the hockey team. He is known for his fast speed and brilliant ability to outwit the opposing team. His team won the National Championship.

Dillon, the break dancer. When the neighborhood kids challenged him to breakdance, he beat them all. The way Dillon moves, you would think he was born to dance. Dillon is fearless and he is confident in what he does!

Peyton and Paige, the fastest readers in class. They've been reading since they were a year old. That's amazing!

There's Brooker and his singing group, the future next Top American Superstars. They can really sing! My feet get to moving and fingers get to snapping and my head get to bopping. Somebody please call the police because I need stopping!

Marlow is the quietest kid in school, but when he smiles, he brightens up the whole classroom. Marlow does not talk much, but his actions speak louder than words.

Clipper is what you call the most popular boy in the whole school. He knows a lot of stuff. He's always on the run to learn more interesting things that no one knows yet.

Sunny Trae Jackson, a.k.a. the best and coolest dresser in the school. He always wore the newest styles.

What do you think is going on with David?
Let's talk about it.

Do you see yourself in any one of these kids that David wanted to be like? Do you think David will find himself in this story?

Keep reading . . . turn to the next page.

There was a girl named Maya. Her mother named her after the great poet, Maya Angelou. Like the great poet, she had a zest and passion for poetry. When she recited poetry, the audience would stand up on their feet, applauding with amazement and enjoyment. She singlehandedly mesmerized the audience and brought them to tears. Her performance was outstanding.

There was a commercial on TV for a special drink and song called "Be Like Mike". The song was about Michael Jordan to be exact. Jordan was the best basketball player of all time. The drink was supposed to make you just like him if you drank it! David thought about the song. He realized that wanting to be like that person doesn't make you that person. The most important thing is to be yourself, not wishing to be anyone else.

Looks like David is
finally on to something.
What do you think?

Turn to the next page

David took a moment to think about and ponder on the gifts he has: a lovable and awesome personality, lots of friends, and a cool, unique style. He's smart as a whip, able to learn anything he put his mind to. He can sing like a rockstar and has his own dance routine. He's been swimming since he was a baby. He reads well, and writes his own stories which he sometimes shares with his classmates.

The most valuable lesson he learned is to be comfortable in himself and be content in all things. David realizes that it is awesome to be him and not what someone else wants him to be.

Everybody is special in their own way and was born with their own unique gifts to be a blessing to the world. You can only be the best you. No one can walk in your shoes that are meant for you, nor can you walk in theirs.

I was born to be me and I am awesome being me!

YOU ARE SPECIAL JUST THE WAY YOU ARE!

Think about what
makes you special . . .

...and embrace that with all your heart...

www.ingramcontent.com/pod-product-compliance
Ingram Content Group UK Ltd.
Pitfield, Milton Keynes, MK11 3LW, UK
UKHW061032310726
14089UKWH00009B/213
9798218326227